I Understand

Understanding Others

Rosie McKee

SOCIAL AND EMOTIONAL LEARNING FOR THE REAL WORLD™

Rosen Classroom™

My friend is sad.

I know how it feels to be sad.

She needs a hug.
I understand.

She needs to cry.
I understand.

She needs to talk.
I understand.

I know how she feels.
I understand.

Words to Know

cry

hug